TANGERINE

or, how I learned to trust the process

TANGERINE

or, how I learned to trust the process

By

Joey Groves

Grooovy Books

First published in Great Britain 2021

A CIP catalogue record for this book is available
from the British Library

ISBN: 978-1-8382116-2-2

www.grooovy.co

To my father, Chris

Contents

TANGERINE

or, how I learned to trust the process

Solace

anything is better than here
just longing for you
waiting for the embrace
and the fear of losing
a face of outright neutrality
assuming that, you, my darling:
the touch that's raising my heart
beats for you are choosing eternity
over me

the world you've seen now
it's inside your psychedelically
green eyes
don't worry, i see!
wishing how you managed
to slither your soul into my
jumpy heart
though i can see that your prize
is getting cold -
it's your favourite after all
i'd love to see you once again:
once for now

we shall see,

trying to find solace

Lost in the waves

Lost in the waves
I'm just counting down the ways
Things could've turned out
waiting on you to give me a shout

Trouble

You look like the kinda trouble
I wouldn't mind getting into

Head down, keepin' on mumbling
I couldn't really find myself;
shedding you from my gaunt skeleton.
Hoping it would have led to catharsis;
the way things are heading,
the exuberance you gave me
in that short period of time -
I will echo for myself

As if I nonchalantly
fall in love once again
(soon)

Under The Spotlight

As hard it is to say
It is the only way; my dear
Our love, is madly incapable
That is
because it is inescapable
Do you hear?

Your love: as deep, vast and natural
Like the unknown ocean
It is mine to keep
And yours to breathe
And ours to discover
Whereas, my love: bleak, outcast and
unilateral
It is mine to weep
And you the bourgeoisie
We need each other

Time is upright
My yearning; stupefied
Your luscious locks that
radiates incandescently as do
The Golden constellations above
Unlocked;

Over the bright blue trees
and purple skies
She lies
A face of a goddess:
Shining bright with moonlight
with ties of burgundy;
the delights of blue

Under the spotlight: you and me
Together 'till eternity

a time before your eyes

a time before your eyes;
swirling as a
night sky arise from dusk

lips plump, so tempting
but the boss says:
"I can't"
but I can tempt Cupid
with an arrow

As a Georgia peach
pink with promise
for soul mates

Similar to mines,
I have a 60s soul,
so will you come with me
and speak my language?

I don't know enough
to tell you

Something

It's something you don't think of much.
Her eyes the colour of the ocean
mixed in with the greys of my socks.
It pierces through my
sunken soul
and anchors itself in my sleep.

Her love is mine to keep.
Nevertheless,
it's her touch that seems
to make me breathe.
It's another life
but somehow everything's the same.

I'm older,
and I should be living
through many adventures.
But it seems that my clock's
ticking faster than other people's;
I don't know why
but my heart can be very cold.
I get really angry
and irrational and yet still go on,
but how many more before the toll of it
all hits me?

It's just how I deal with it -
my feet are on fire.
The bags under my eyes:
I look tired.

I saw you today

I saw you today,
You looked even more beautiful
Than usual
I don't know if you saw me
but if you did
You probably noticed that my
Pupils swelled up to the size of
the moon
Or how my natural almond pigment
turned Rosy
Or how I forgot to blink and breath:
so did my heart

I'm beatific
You're my heart's
yearning and gravity
Your sun-kissed blonde hair
tied up, to look like the stars itself
Through my round shaped glasses:
the moon

Who would have known?

twisting and turning

twisting and turning
oh my heart's yearning
how are we still here?
i fear we've past each other

different highs or lows
i never got to show
how i'd love her
when i've been waiting for her

isn't it a joke
how we met?
we shouldn't have!
though my memory's
gone instead

i've fallen out of love,
you're the one who broke *it*
never in a million years
would i expect,
that you,
of all people
would shatter *it* into pieces

All that I miss is in you

All that I miss is in you
Contemplating about existence
But nothin ain't working
because none of it matters
but you

Looking like a fool, missing
my friends and my family
Am I making a good person
out of myself?

Or am I making a fool?
Love's all we give,
however, missing you it shall

Existential Dread

I want to be something,
but I don't know *What*.
To do one thing,
that I do not.

Grey

A grey eyed
woman
or a girl
with many strengths

There are days
where I think about you;
how you wispfully grace around my thoughts

I care about you,
where your shame
is mine to bear
and mine is mine only

My mental health be trippin' sometimes
but that doesn't matter
because I've put all my love
and worth into you

It's a loss,
but it's something
I'm willing to do
(It's dumb)

You want what I want,
separated by countys and roads

Loneliness

Loneliness got the best of me
it doesn't help that sleep deprivation
got a hold of me
I'm infatuated but, also, I'm in a rush
I don't know why
It's as if death would come
bursting out the door and
slice me into a million little
pieces, until the end of time

oh how i have longed to feel

oh how i have longed to feel,
in eternity, this other worldly being
i crush and i fall for you:
my sweet

i am a realist;
i don't expect you to
carry my heart
and leave
but if truth is ever
hazed
then i shall
tumble and forget
(soon;)
for i do not have the time
to wallow in miasma
not again
(not again)

i feel your aura
with me:
an apparition holding my hand,
through the love that is thick!
if the sun has faded away
i will try to make it shine
don't you worry
there's nothing i wouldn't do
for you

do you want the moon?
when my body is close to you,
i shall tie up a lasso
and cast the rope
hoping the purple sky
would bite
and the moon shall be yours

if the flowers dance,
the water whispering,
clouds swooning
and the bumble bee
shaking its bum,
to the rhythm of a
swiss railway watch
(tick tick)

it is fate
that works in
such uncanny ways

i'm a fool
if i don't love

All my words

All my words
I find
for something
you hear

I heard that
I was in your heart.
Ummm the thing is
that I left it all
behind for you,
I wish I gave you the love
you clearly deserved

Instead I left you:
a stupid joke

10am

It's getting hard to pretend
when I intend to
move away from the scene

And, personally, it seems
to develop one's self is a burden -
when her then,
was more than
a ten
in my eyes,
I wish it was all lies

Smiles all around
When I'm miles a bound
to make lives
easier.

I don't know anything:
if only
being lonely
improved our chakras

I'm scared of the future;
and never amounting to anything,
or never reaching my full potential
I'm scared of being inadequate
and being left behind

I hate feeling dumb.

Control

Control, it was theirs
making me feel paranoid
thinking it was fair
for me to go through

Most of life
sick and annoyed
Thus it was written:
trauma...
home has spoken.

Only then I was finding
a way out
	to open one's self
to the critic that
lies between Earth and Mars.

What an arse!

A friend

A friend says I've got big heart -
cold
inside,
I'm packed
full of myself.

Love possesses me.
I'm a hopeless romantic,
is my soul intact?

A friend says I've got a big heart
cold,
narcissistic tendencies hold over me.
The tin man's shy,
my heart's hacked into
pieces: by my own self.

Love possesses me.
I'm a recovering love addict,
my soul,
stuck in a tar pit of my ways.

A stranger tells me,
    that I need to take it easy
    as he devours
    a pack of cigarettes
    and a cup of coffee

There was time

there was time,
before i knew you,
life was riddled with mistimings
and stupid decisions -
climbing away:
in fear of losing it all

from a young age
actions were petitions
to show my affinity (okay)
mostly wishing it were true
instinctually i've been saying
i've been alright for the longest
knowing you,
you wouldn't leave me astray

Choosing!
Here or there
Love is a fool's game
Only then, they realise
Easy goes
Grooving all over the place
Enchantingly graced
Over me, yet hung up
Ready to charge through the
light brigade

Going places, hoping to get somewhere
Instant jealousy
Never even got the best of me
Adjacent to you is:
Me, one and everywhere
Elegies
Looking for
Amusement within
Nights filled with spools of
Intentions filled with goodness - who knows?!

Elegant;
Yet so so malaise

Harking

It just happened
At some point,
We got lost in the waves,
but whenever we cross paths
I feel like I'm being saved
I'm scared of it ending
because it just barely
started

I feel like I'm using you;
I don't know
(or remember)
half of the things
I've spewed
out of my mouth:
Harking

But I know I'm in the wrong
and I'm unfair to myself
because this should have
never happened
in the first place

I'm happy you're here
And I hope you'll still be there
and I rest my case

Summer love

Summer love
it isn't real.
Being childish doesn't
make you feel,
But I was shoving words
I want to say to you
down my throat
I'm tired(ish)
of doing that

you're childish
        like me
Asking for toys for Christmas
when we're both nineteen
Nerdy, geeky or whatever
you want to call it.
We like the same things

Is your eyesight so poor like mine?
Afterall we're short sighted,
I think

Tomorrow

tomorrow i'm in
the sunken place
time's a tickin',
one hour after the other

cold summers
so the flowers never bloom
rather
the tongue can say
endless flowing words
that'll end up in a paper cup;
damn you're getting dumber,
acting like a goon

tomorrow is another day
speak up and have ur say

Summer Sun

Summer sun's up
It's the other house
It's always been rough kid
You're just good at ignoring it

Playing in the sun for hours
Playing video games for hours
Playing life

Now you're here:
I'm getting more responsibility
and I feel more insecure and less confident
How did I get here?

I just wanna go home
I just wanna go home

Polaroids

She's got my polaroids
on her wall.

We got strawberry
and chocolate crepes
at the mall.

Watching the sunset,
while drowning
(she thinks I'm bipolar)

Always lying in bed
doubting myself
(drinking Coca Cola)

Weird

Why are you so weird?
What do you fear
My boy?
Everything will be alright;
Keep telling yourself that

ABSURD

'I'll prolly die anonymous
I'll prolly die with promises...
Or maybe die from panic or die from bein' too lax
Or die from waitin' on it, die 'cause I'm movin' too fast...
I'll prolly die 'cause that's what you do when you're 17
All worries in a hurry, I wish I controlled things'

- Kendrick Lamar
Pulitzer Prize Winner

Death (Mortir)

What happened when death
came knocking down my door
I did nothin'
I stood there watchin'
My mother in front of me
shaking rigorously from the cold:
death put inside her.

She called me like twenty times,
before I came.
Plugged in to my music,
earphones on,
typing away.

When I came
she was close to death -
the boy who cried wolf,
the tragedy is that no one came
and helped.
That was me for the longest

I called Dad up
from downstairs
and told him to call the ambulance,
she was colder by the hour
her soul sucked out and frozen.

The ambulance came quick
but it felt like an eternity
I just stood there,
just wasting away,
needed to distract myself
so I started typing away,
she's gone.

Dad followed,
I'm all alone,
I called up Mary and
bawled my eyes out.

Scared and lonely,
she was also there too,
she cheered me up.
I'm glad she was there.

Stayed up all night writing away,
Dad came back at 1am,
while I pretended to sleep.

It was Rigor,
that she suffered through.
Five minutes later it would have
been Mortis.

No Exit

is there anyone out there listening?
or am i just screaming into the void?
am i crazy for dreaming the things
i've thought?
things outside the box?
i need to talk to tyler, frank or ye because
i'm feeling so lost
can you call me sometime?
leave me a voicemail
i'll put it on the album
"listening"
i feel like i'm screaming into the void

FUCK

FUCK
  ME
AND
  MY MIND
  MY MENTAL
      HEALTH IS
      FUCKING
      KILLING
      ME

ears-a ringin

ears-a ringin
i'm wishing i wasn't so anxious at this moment
running into you kinda caught me off guard
melancholy smiles got me fakin to my friends
that i'm alright
melancholy eyes've got my fam'ly thinkin'
to turn a blind eye

my Momma almost died
one time, i was typing my essay
panicking because the deadline was the next day
she called for me, once,
i didn't answer
headphones plugged in
typing away
she called me again
i shouted back at her
with a short fuse in the tone
of my voice
i half slammed the door so
i can get on with my stupid essay

the last scream
"shit! something's wrong"
as if death was engulfing her vocal chords.
eventually,
i pull my headphones out -
walked heavy footed towards the sound
of desperation

Here.
She is barely audible.
There.
She's twitching as if she was possessed
by an evil entity.
Everywhere.
Tossing, turning, holding back screeches
of death
(from even in her last moments,
she was holding back to protect me)

I ran downstairs,
told my Dad there's something wrong with Mum
I shout at him, I never do, to call the ambulance.

Thank God they got here in time.
If we left it any longer, there wouldn't be...
Dad packed a bunch of her clothes and rushed to the
hospital with her
I was left, in the house on my own,
clothes and bags scattered everywhere

I'm overwhelmed with everything
I continue typing
i keep lying to myself
I joke
because humour is all i know

Rock Bottom

Missing everything
I miss my old friends
   I miss talking to them
I miss the feeling when I'm with them
My room's not a safe haven anymore

I miss feeling confident in myself
now I feel like a failure
I feel like I don't know
myself anymore
I pushed away my friends
I pushed away myself
I'm not good anymore
I'm lazy
   My mind's filled with haze
I'm filled with so much hate
I miss the feeling of happiness
that comes along with confidence

This *is* the absence of God's love
I need answers
    this is hell

And I have to write this
down quick
because I don't remember
so well.

What have I become?

Heart's been in pieces

Heart's been in pieces
Just can't help thinkin'
she is there for me
But am I there for her?
Common sense been shrinkin
Ever since
I've been coming,
tense, frustrated.

Mama told me
to get some more sleep
But to be honest
I ain't been doing anything
I'm just wastin' away
Wish I was a better
person truly.

Rolling Down

I'm rolling down,
deep into the
smoke rings

Twisting
on the one hand
on the other
just being engulfed
by a frame

Out of town,
feeling as lonely
as I've ever been

Switching between
one vice to another:
DAMN.

Wandering around the house,
if only you'd get it
A way of self-induced therapy
Emotions on a page
Sorrows and moods in a hue
Selfish in part
but I'm willing to share
to the world

The breed doesn't phase me
Collaboration marks the paper cup
My mind's still hazy

For a few,
it's how they hide
dirty laundry
in the cupboard

Give it a shake:
the ignorance and subtlety of
ignoring a vagrant

Delusions

Feeling like everybody's
Out there to get me
Times like these
Make me wonder
Was I born lucky?
Or was I lucky to be born?

It's painful to be born
It's painful to die
Whilst suffering,
living
all the time

Kill your creativity!

My heart aches from sorrow

My heart aches from sorrow
hoping there's better days to come
tomorrow
my head's been in a daze
feeling like I haven't been
myself, sent myself on the craze
for a minute or two
Just wanted to be out of my bag
But this bad acid
damagin my kinfolk

I feel nothing
absolutely nothing

Sorrowful clouds,
me, like a lizard
pitter pattering
on top of a pond

But everything's okay
I'm just hurt because
Hope hoped that my
intuitions were wrong
(But like everything else in life
my intuitions were right)

Paranoid

Hollow,
Is how I feel
whenever you're not around.
Feels like forever
since we've talked

Followed,
by everyone
and I'm freaking out,
got some time -
back in my bag

Oh no
the high's waning
and i'm waiting
infatuated with
finally being inside
these walls:

Sis
I've been trying
but it's not getting easier
Rue's been telling what to do
(all my life)
but I'm sick of following rules:
I just want to be real
For once I wish I'm not
the fool

Ode to Mum

Sleeping in
my memories of
cold winters:
Mum's cuddles
and kisses
fighting along
with me
against the
dark mornings, days
and evenings

Dark weeks
are hard to tolerate
Easy to bleed
my mind's meek
open my teeth
my smile's weak
my eyes tell it

I would tell you
but I wouldn't
want you
to worry

Limbo

Limbo
Did you think Johnny fitted in though?
'Cos back in Chrimbo
Everything wasn't really in show

I've been here before,
Beth was here before
Sitting on the floor
Cross legged,
telling me everything will be
ok -
she was sure
but that's all I needed at the time
I just wish I'd stop being short sighted
and losing people that I
need!

Limbo
Now that I've been cold
hearted, I'm starting to open up
and maybe I'll have my own
kinfolk

it's been a while
since we last spoke
i've been telling lots of jokes
and i'm glad you didn't sigh
much

now that i'm fixing a hole
i hope you'll be around
and we can grow together more
and we can hopefully sing more
folky songs like this

I wanna go home

I just want to go 'home'
and where's that little boy gone?
He wasn't involved with his parents'
drama,
He was very good in school.
He had an innocent smile on his face.
He fell easily in love.
He was quite happy a lot of the time.
He was spoilt
(in love and wealth).
He wasn't self-conscious.
He made people laugh and smile.
He loved.
Even though,
He didn't know everything around
him was broken.

And eventually,
everything would catch up with him,

So did he.

Crabbing

Ocean's fly
Seaside
Legs hangin'
Buckets happenin'

Love is present
Bacon tied up
to a prisoner of dreams
Did you know rocks are crescents
but who's really shy?
enough is enough!
Snakes are a hissin' behind the scenes

I flip
and I flop
I drip
and I drop
Kids smile
I'm free?

I guess Dad was right.

goodbye

goodbye
separating ourselves
for my own good
and to tell
the truth
i'm okay without you

it breaks my heart
to see us grow apart
but what can i do?
us and our youth
those days are behind us
maybe minus
the heartbreaks -
for now

i paid for this,
for my dreams
and growth.
now that it is:
nothing is what it seems

broken promises
and late night conversations;
flipped a switch in your head
it's like you went on vacation
and you left me behind

oh my
why do you have to be so far?

Diss stance

I want you
The distance does kill us
It's something I've been
ignoring
(I'm a dreamer after all)
I know I can be stubborn
and a little bit sus
But -

I just hope you don't think we're boring

Telephone Love

I'm in awe of you
and of our
medium too;
it's not enough
it doesn't serve
what we've been through

Does my love mean anything to you?

Does my love mean anything to you?
Or is it stuck in the past like everything else?

Loops

Going 'round,
in cycles,
and loops.

That's what
makes sense
and doesn't

I keep going around
in circles
never learning

Fried

Feel in the cloud
the cloud that is depression

how did i drink that glass of water?
did i turn on the lights?

time is solace
it's phases
and loops

one minute
we're high

one minute
we're paranoid

and it's done
and it goes again
and we forget

it's a self deprecating loop

Home

Home is a wonderful thing
that not a lot of people have
the true comfort of saying
they truly have;
not behind a prison cell
or a desk in a cubicle

To me,
I selfishly declare,
is the warmth of my mother's embrace,
my father's loving heart,
my friend's support
and my own will
and determination

That's what home
is to me

I feel as tho,
I've felt 'all'
of home
but
(not really)

Believing in myself

Love

Love.
It is all I know
therefore all I write
"Will she love me?"
When all I needed
was me.

I needed some sleep for sure

Love is a concept
Just go with the flow
No need to rush because
life is a
surprise

and life is
HOME

2:40am

Today, everything came to an end:
I've got closure on a lot of things
and it felt good

Yet,
I'm yearning
for more

I'm anxious about my future,
my exams:
I want to do well

I feel lonely
but hopeful

Overall, I do
feel hopeful
and motivated
    it's just sad:
    the people, the place

It's sad!!

But I shall
feel solace
soon,

Because I'm starting to believe in myself
and I feel...
LOVED

falling in love isn't that bad

falling in love isn't that bad
at some point,
when you're falling
and falling
you shouldn't feel so sad

toss a coin
and figure it out
because one day
it won't be a fad

Cartridge

Holding on for dear life
in your hands.
I would get the flowers
and polka dots to sing
for you

Dreaming too much
but I had a smile
That's one thing
I'd spend hours doing:
just making songs
about you

Silly as they come
no one really saw us
Laughing at the others
for being absurd

Ironically,
people were probably
batting an eye,
when they saw us laughing
and a snort here and there

Maybe it was too short.
We should have been
in it -
in each other's lives
for an extra minute
but I've enjoyed
the time we've been given,
faffing about with our bags

Of course!
There were fireworks
but the fuse was almost lit,
what a long journey it's gonna be
at least I'm in shorts
I've got my keys,
we're driving

Yet I'm going so soon
and you too
Wishing it was the way I wanted
but you don't really care

It's magic, it's love, it's the movies

Sister

Distant flowers turn East
for a weekend or so
People slide, they meet
People hide, they eat

What is there to do
but to show
(my heart)
((needed to go))
the hour marches
yet the butterfly beats

Can't you tell?
it's
all well
Flies surround my bag

The plight of the older man
seems so far removed
from today:
"We only have today"

What is it that
our paths reach
for sometime
other than now?

Twist 'N Shout

my hopes twists away
dreaming that i get there
lying staring at the ceiling,
i pray
mustering up delusions;
i dare
tomorrow i shall blow the candles
from my cake
and hope i get there

it would be a shame
if i don't
i don't even know what i'd do:
i want it bad

1 am

Oh, umm.
I don't know
There are words
that pop up but
there are none when I see you
Not because of the non-chalant
greeting I gave because
I was happy to see you
no no!
it was me trying to conceal
my inner joy:
fireworks
(exploding inside me)

what is said in the spaces are
all that's ever known.

But the what ifs
(and or buts)
we want to say
each other
stays locked inside us
for eternity

I write about what
I know and
I know that
I wanna see you
and spend every waking
moment with you

Yet,
I don't know
what to say.

The best thing I can
say is some nonsense
gobbledygook
because I'll find myself
in that
(Body and Soul)

I know these things aren't easy.
And that's the best thing I can do
No one really expects much from you
(they only expect, what you show)

Expectations can crumble
a man

And so, it did

loving you ain't that easy

loving you ain't that easy
you're the kinda
trouble
i wouldn't mind
getting into
i just want you to kiss me,
so baby,
will you wait for me
i'll be there in
a little while

silly lil love poems

tell me are you here?
or are you bare?

people keep telling me
i'm alright
but my insides
are tearing me apart -
it's no fun

i'm willing to put up a fight
but how many times
do i have to get back up?
run away;
my instinct dives
into cold water

failing within cycles
or loops
where it matters

opening my heart
is scary
it's something
i don't understand;
the fallout greater than the feelin'
inside

with regards
to my logic
i'm just being alive

love is a process

love is a process
love is a passion

Cranberry Juice

(I don't get it)
I had dreams here,
naïveté or hope
call it whatever
one thing
i was
conquering was:
fear

Why doesn't she love me man?
I would have ran away
to the ends of the Earth
with her

But little did I
know

it's late there

it's late here
laying in my bed
wishing i was cuddling you
sometimes i fear
you don't feel the same
but it might just be
in my head
my heart's beating
(it's not the anxiety)
i'm just alive
i trust fate
and myself

i wish i was back
to the place
where i found home
and read about
your heinous love:
you and the comrades,
togetherness is not a fool -
bread baking in the oven

just the feeling of home
(more of the blues)
rolling down my cheek
it's late here and it
isn't the same
it's bleak -
it's really cooking
the timer's ticking

all i feel is that
of your aura
and i'd be the opposite.
if you go,
if he's there for you,
i'll let you go

do the stars in the sky
ever feel the warmth
you give me?
though the moon has
a dark side
it's always there for you/me.

whenever it's raining
you're the calming
lo-fi piano playing inside me -
wanting and waning for me to
curl up in a soft, freshly washed blanket;
reading a book
(the paper crisp)
and a fresh cup
of hot chocolate oozing out
its sweet scent
longing for you;

soft marshmallows kissing my lips.
reminiscent of that
i used to nuzzle:
my own
sweet heart

Train of Thoughts

I was just thinking
People really do peculiar things
Like the fact
we long for one another
yet we feel the loneliness
that permeates through the universe;
maybe in a paper cup

Boy, do I pour my heart out,
but what for?
I keep digging for something?

I've come across gold
and other precious metals
yet I long for something more -
someone like you

Protective, jealous guy
only one of us to reach the sky
Your eyes concentrated on the illumination
of your bright tinsel

But what about the season?
    it's alright,
no more keeping
secrets;
though execution by treason
doesn't seem pleasant
It'll hurt less with
you holding the axe

Lying little dace,
wishing I was flying
Forcing myself through
the thick waning facade
of your brittle little soul

Yet I'm here giving out
all my whole
hearted angst.
Zealots coming for my hair,
wondering
where I can go
I wish I told you sooner
but oh so help me
I'm stuck
in my insufficient ways

Hoping I'd be ruled
futile by her
You're more than
what I asked for
Then again,
I don't ask for a lot -
no, that's a lie.

It's a shame I knew you
before you knew me.
Don't you wish you were
someone else?
Because I would rather be wearing a mask

Ask yourself really?
It's when you're over there,
only then, the paper runs out
but the traitor always gets away,
he wins, yet he kills with a smile

Does he?
Or does she?
It's all over
the place is a tranquil space
For you
but not for me

The Midas touch for pain,
I'd rather just be.
Always paying and making amends
It's such a drag,
so what is there?
Love?
That is all I know but
I do not know
how to receive
such a thing
as love

So please teach me
(It's futile)

Winter Sun

The winter sun's riding low
everything seems to be glowing

Spirits

Spirits of days past
still lingers in me
when I'm in this house;
spirits of insecurity,
guilt, jealousy, "love",
lust, trust, distance.

I'm all alone
in my thoughts
in the same
shower
where I had
my first panic attack

Today, I'm wanting to text you
but I can't think of anything to say
so I won't force it

Feelin' so empty
Pretty faces swirling
Inside a year of healing
Been inside for a minute
I'm so lonely;
eaten up like an empty yoghurt pot

She
ain't
giving me
attention

Tangerine

Soft spoken,
she reminds me of home
Thought that I was open
but I had some demons of my own

Time was the truth,
I should have been me,
at least pretending to be,
instead of acting
as if I'm not broken
or aloof

I moaned;
like all the time
Stubborn in my ways,
should have combed my hair
before going away

(Damn!
I need to buy
some milk;
I'm baking a cake)

I've shown you I care
Now it's your turn to
pick up the phone:
Just a thought to bare

Saying goodbye to a piece of home

Saying goodbye to a piece of home
is always hard

When I'm with them,
I'm lonely

When they're gone,
I'm lonely

No one's really listening
but I'm just screaming
into the void

I don't regret
my confessions of love
because it's just a toy

But I'm slowly learning
to love myself

Time

Time considers your wishes and curses -
for it is fair

While your heart's mending
in stitches,
an old soul is asking for time
to slow down -
as time is picking up its pace
(to mend your shore)

For a care in the world,
you shouldn't wish for
time to pick
a side

It shows you a lesson
otherwise heard from
Mother or Father

What love is loss?

Moments

if only we
had longer moments

if only
we could say everything to each other -
in those spaces;
our thoughts,
while cars chase their dreams;
our insecurities on to other people
and people you might not ever meet;
then
 i'd say how much i truly love you

Dreaming

It's about being scared
and doing it anyway

Am I wrong in dreaming
and having ambitions
of my own?

'I'd rather chase things
never thought of'

It shouldn't be this hard
but it is

Sweet Baby Boy

Sweet baby boy
you don't have to lie
(anymore)
everything will be alright

Crooked teeth
seeing snow
(for the first time)

Falling

Things keep falling apart
so we always
keep readjusting

(There's beauty in the attempt)
So I just have to:
Trust the Process

A letter to my 15 year old self

It's bad right now
Let yourself hurt for a bit

Things will be fine tomorrow
just keep telling yourself that

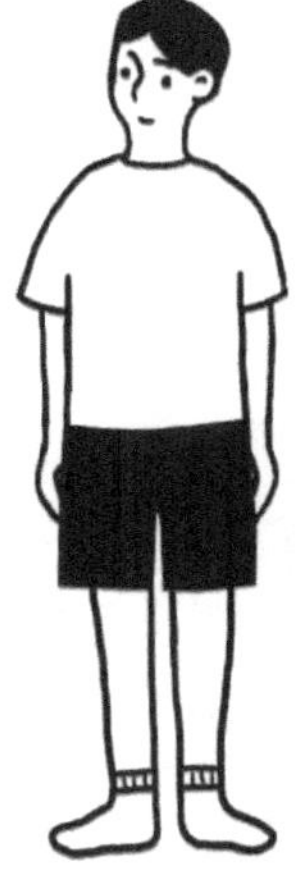

Notes

'A friend': the poem contains a line from Earl Sweatshirt's song, 'Solace': 'stuck in a tar pit of my ways'.

'Tomorrow': 'sunken place' is in reference to the hypnotic, trance-like state the protagonist is put under in the 2017 film, 'Get Out'.

'Polaroids': the poem interpolates lyrics from King Krule's song, 'Biscuit Town': 'I think she thinks I'm bipolar'.

'No Exit': the poem's title is taken from Jean-Paul Sartre's 1944 existentialist play of the same name.

'Rolling Down': 'DAMN.' is in reference to Kendrick Lamar's 2017 Pulitzer Prize winning album.

'My heart aches from sorrow': the poem interpolates lyrics from Earl Sweatshirt's song, 'December 24': 'Bad apple, daily clashing with my kinfolk/ Bad acid did damage to my mental'.

'Twist 'N Shout': the poem's title is in reference to The Beatles' cover of 'Twist and Shout'.

'Dreaming': the poem contains a brief quotation from Childish Gambino's song, 'III. Life: The Biggest Troll [Andrew Auernheimer]'.

Acknowledgements

I would like to thank the editors of Soul Talk Magazine
for publishing some of these poems for the first time:
'Tomorrow', 'Harking' and 'Solace' in Issue 02:
Isolation (2020, August).

Thank you also to my parents for raising me right,
for supporting all of my crazy and ambitious ideas
and helping me close this chapter in my life. I am so
grateful.

To my extraordinary friends, for believing in me and
pushing me to become a better person. You know who
you are. I can't begin to describe how lucky I am to
have you in my life. You are my rock.

To my therapist, who helped me face my trauma and
prompted my process of healing.

To the teachers and professors who've inspired me.

And to Bo Burnham, Donald Glover, Kendrick Lamar,
Mac Demarco, Archy Marshall and John Lennon.

And Elke. Thank you for being my creative backbone.

– Joey Groves

Acknowledgments

To Joey,

Who let me be a part of his creative process, and trusted me with the responsibility of making the packaging for his years of emotion, experience, and artistry put to paper.

I have no doubt that you'll manage to ignite the poetry flame to many more people, like you did to me.

And above all, thanks for making this process so much fun.

– Elke

Joey Groves is a writer, poet, musician and software engineer. He released his first full-length album 'The Earlyman Tape' in 2019 under the stage name Liddypool.

When Joey isn't writing, he can be found listening to The Beatles or Childish Gambino, making music, watching YouTube videos, playing video games, and hanging out with his friends.

www.grooovy.co